SMALL BOAT
WITH OARS OF DIFFERENT SIZE

SMALL BOAT WITH OARS OF DIFFERENT SIZE

Poems by
Thom Ward

Carnegie Mellon University Press
Pittsburgh 2000

Acknowledgments

Grateful acknowledgment is made to the editors of these journals and newspapers where many of the poems, or earlier versions of them, have appeared: *Acorn Whistle:* "Going on the Belief Walleyes Eat Late"; *Aethlon:* "Everywhere, Pachysandra"; *The Alaska Quarterly Review:* "The Woman with a Full Tank"; *The American Literary Review:* "Dark Underfoot"; *The Atlantic Monthly:* "Vasectomy"; *The Christian Science Monitor:* "Each Saturday After"; *Clackamas Literary Review:* "As This Is Our Century"; *Confrontation:* "White Birds"; *Connecticut River Review:* "Black Forests"; *Desperate Act:* "Anaphoric" and "On Being Kicked Out of the Harold Washington Library Center for Napping on the Floor"; *The Dickinson Review:* "God's Enigmatic Silence"; *The Eleventh Muse:* "Shopping with Henry David Thoreau"; *Exquisite Corpse:* "Swimmers"; *Loonfeather:* "Water Baby"; *Lynx Eye:* "Early Morning Cafeteria Orchestra"; *Many Mountains Moving:* "The Bar Beyond the World"; *Onion River Review:* "In the Interest of Possibility"; *Poet Lore:* "Faster"; *Prairie Schooner:* "Stray Dogs, Foaming"; *Press:* "Regarding Shoulders" and "The Man with a New Toothbrush"; *Rain City Review:* "Spin Cycle"; *River Oak Review:* "While We Rest"; *Salamander:* "The Revisionist at Work"; *Tar River Poetry:* "Hunting Skunk Cabbage," "The End Won't Be So Bad," and "Condiments"; *The Texas Observer:* "Bon Voyage"; *Yankee:* "Only the Traveler Can Change the Journey" and "Sandy Lake, Late August"; *Yellow Silk:* "Walking Down This Mountain," "Barbara," and "Honeysuckle Bower."

Poems from this collection have appeared in the following anthologies: *New Voices* (Colorado State University), *Outsiders* (Milkweed Editions), *Prayers to Protest* (Pudding House), *The 1997 Anthology of Magazine Verse & Yearbook of American Poetry* (Monitor Book Company), *Poetry: An Introduction* and *The Bedford Introduction to Literature* (Bedford Books / St. Martin's Press).

The Publication of this book is supported by a grant from the Pennsylvania Council on the Arts.

Contents

SPIN CYCLE

for **Barbara**
lighthouse & buoy

Stray Dogs, Foaming

Hunting Skunk Cabbage

we need patience and boots
glazed with saddle soap. The ground
is always wet. Patches of ice don't help
as we wander during the flash of a thaw,
find old cattails, deer pellets,
cans and papers snared in thorns,
if we're lucky one woolly starfish
of mullein. But no skunk cabbage.
So, we return, say, in late March,
because they can't hide forever.
We walk. Blackbirds tick.
Clouds tattooed with geese
try to distract our vision
which we've got to keep forward
and down. *There.* In a muddied swale,
through a clump of moss, the mottled bronze
shoves. This one is a scout with a spathe and bracts,
fancy terms for botanists, for us
it means spring. The throat, slender as a swan's,
could break: so my wife pets it gently,
says the texture is sponge, no, more like rubber.
I watch her run a finger up the tip—
and for god sake's—the plant squeaks.
That's what we hear. Not the wind
or the moan of trampled leaves,
but the squeaking herds of cabbage
twisting from puddles and melt,
stretching their throats in the crisp air,
parading the round, green flowers,
knobbed like grenades, that she absolutely
refuses to touch. When crushed,
it's the foulest of odors. I take her hand,
and we wait another minute as the mud

works our boots and purple horns
bump the earth. Skunk cabbage,
Symplocarpus foetidus, arriving to remind us
it doesn't matter what is buried
compared to what is pushing through.

Dark Underfoot

The impulse among us is to throw eyes
skyward. Shaggy heads of maples,
the summer's blue turban, we tug
the sleeve of another as kestrels
float over fields. Icarus and Earhart.
At night in our rooms cherubs assemble,

hover like little dirigibles,
our last thought the space
from Adam's finger to God's touch.
The infant looks up toward the breast,
and the man in the open casket
watches satellites drift

across the back of his lids. What
can we say about the ruts
in the old, dirt road? No one
paints the apostles on sidewalks.
Children freeze before cellar steps.
Maybe our blindness is astral, snow-capped,

and wandering we miss
the mushrooms' inveterate work.
More Light! More Light! Goethe cried.
And so do we. But who will trace
what is dark underfoot?
Who will wait for the nightcrawler to sing?

Shopping with Henry David Thoreau

So
we roam the bulk foods
as I'm trying to school him
on double-saver coupons,
how we don't buy
for the whole damn winter,
how our days are spent in quest
of frosted Pop Tarts, Kraft
macaroni and cheese, that smart
shoppers use pagan spells to summon
industrious elves, those little Keeblers
who bake our cookies stuffed
with polyunsaturated fats, gum sorbate,
the recommended daily allowance of riboflavin,
but he's not listening, those gray, goshawk eyes
aren't steeled on the frozen
Swanson entree I'm holding.
No, he's zeroed in on Grandma Brown, wants
to telegraph the bespectacled and kind,
(and very much dead), leguminous matriarch.
And he's miffed, can't find directions
to her farm on the label, can't extrapolate
if she plants beans deep in rows,
if the same enemies—crawlers, woodchucks,
crunch her crop for lack of johnswort.
He wants answers and so asks me:
What has she learned of beans?
Is she busy about them? How,
under the laws binding the firmament,
has this woman grown
sugar cane in eastern woodlands?
It's enough to make his brow runnel
like the furrows he digs, his face

the color of McIntosh.
From her perch above the label, Grandma says
nothing, her secrets nitrogen-rich,
her coy, molasses grin
that is so disturbing, displeasing,
to his excellency, the bean king,
to Hank.

Condiments

I don't like it when people use big words.
It's mayonnaise language.
They spread those words like mayonnaise over bread.
　　　　　　　　　　　　　　　　　　　—Peter, age 10

Sorry to bamboozle, but please
liberate the ketchup; we need more
than a dollop for this repast.
While you're at it could you dispense
a smattering of relish, some
vivacious mustard. Commingled
with regal Worcestershire,
they make a delicious pastiche.
Don't forget the irascible salsa,
the rarefied soy, to reave a bottle
of redolent barbecue. Be prepared.
You'll need plenty of chutzpah
to cajole the stolid tartar,
track and snare the horseradish,
that cagey fugitive. Did I mention
it's best to ensconce the hallowed A.1.
until others have proselytized
to lesser toppings? Such felicity
in a synchrony of sauces,
a cavalcade of condiments.
Hurry! We must discharge without delay.
The palate is fickle, the stomach perfidious.
Who knows what machination
they may execute against our fare.

While We Rest

he cleans his room, sifts
through books, games, puzzles,
Ninja Turtles, colored markers,
burbling silly make-up songs.
Hey Mom! His voice comes
through the wall.
Where'd you put my ascension cord?

I don't know sweetie,
try checking beneath your lamp. . . .
most of her body crumpled into sleep.
He goes back to work,
pushing off the nose cones of his sneaks,
stacking what will fit
on cheap, plastic shelves.

When his reach falls short,
he hops, jumps and throws a book
to the top deck, picks up a matchbox car,
hops, jumps and throws again.
Some things in this life stay put.
Our son is not one of them.
From the start his eyes were on

the attic, the trap door of his mother,
she, listless from the spinal.
It must have been then
he first used his ascension cord,
slick with starshine and mud,
to climb from that world
to this. We cannot keep him

out of trees and forts, from leaping
at banners, door frames, basketball nets.
He stands on counters and chairs,
the lip of our neighbor's picket fence—
Look Dad, it's a cinch—hangs like a clothespin
from the school's monkey bars.
So, in the tangle of his room

there is always the chance
he may stumble upon his lost
ascension cord. A magic string,
a secret rope we have never touched,
but would use if he showed us
how to pitch it over the rafters,
chalk our hands, set our grip,
climb fist after fist into the fabulous air.

Bon Voyage

Beginner's luck is the best hope
I can muster in *Navigator*—
a board game rife with famous explorers,

treasures, serpents lurking in uncharted
waters. It's her invention, this game.
She's drawn a map and compass,

seven continents, various trade routes
shoelacing the deep, cerulean seas;
made the smooth bowls of walnut shells

galleons; turned toothpicks, paste
and colored paper into tall sails.
I'm the parent on parents' day,

eager as she explains who rolls when,
who asks what, how to earn points,
how to squander them. We sit on the edge

of our chairs, my daughter, three friends
and I, and plan our strategies—
Pizarro racing Columbus

and Columbus racing da Gama
who's hot to challenge Cabot for furs
or for spice, Marco Polo.

Out of Lisbon, I tack south, southeast
down the Ivory Coast; the seas are gentle;
my responses quick and lead commanding.

I know that Greenland isn't green,
that Drake outfoxed the Armada,
the elusive fountain Ponce de Leon's foil.

Sails fat with wind, confidence
high as the crow's nest, somewhere
around the Cape it goes bad.

I miss question after question—
Henry the Navigator, Eric the Red,
what season the monsoons,

what direction latitudinal lines.
I'm in trouble. The ship's caught
in a net of spidering coral

and scurvy's turned to fever.
Instinct tells me the crew
won't stand for much more.

I've lost time, thirty points and the last
of my chance cards. My daughter says
I've got ten seconds to answer:

Who built the Niña
and the Pinta, but not
the Santa Maria?

Give my cut to the cook,
these letters to my wife.
Boys, she's all yours.

Early Morning Cafeteria Orchestra

The ammonia was louder
than our strings. A half-step sharp,
our teacher held her frown
like a fermata. Week after week
the rest of the kids
attacked each measure as best they could.
But we never improved. Matt,
pasting baseball cards in theory books,
grounded at fifth chair, while I,
urged to challenge Carol and Sue,
faked some of the notes. The world
had long since tried the doctrine
of relativity, which rejects
all absolute truths. Moreover,
it would be years before we'd come
to see our lives as an opus
of exquisite mistakes. Miss Kent
didn't understand, consumed by her talk
of All County. It took something
like skill to fade among
the double basses, the tuba
she'd borrowed from the band.
Practice and more practice,
so many earnest,
little instruments, while Matt
flipped Yankees into his cello case,
and my bow, brilliant with rosin,
went left as the others went right.

Everywhere, Pachysandra

I was told I should give, should sacrifice,
that there was enough country
for boys, fronds, stems, the occasional
tomato garden, enough earth
for mitts, bats, bases,
even mothers with palmate-hearts,
like mine, who, after begonias and mums,

wheeled you out, your pottings
wrapped in peat, and started to dig
the back yard where we played ball.
As I suspected woody plant,
you got most of left field
and the throats of sweet grass.
But by June you were in center,

a green web snagging our grounders
and pop flies. Everything we hit deep
was a twenty-minute ordeal.
Pachysandra chewing, pachysandra moving.
We couldn't stop you, snatching
maple buds, knocking on roots.
You knew what you wanted

and you got it, slick patina
staining our Keds and gloves,
the old Hillerich & Bradsby.
Dusted with sprays, fortified with peat,
you barreled though the rhubarb
and the beans. My mother hunched on fours,
sweating in the August sun,

protected your new pods. She loved you
even though you took Karen's doll,
Ted's decoder ring he left by second base,
went in for juice and that was all.
Day and night, in blistering heat, thunderstorms:
pachysandra chewing, pachysandra moving.
And so it's late. October stars

and the basswood edged gold,
touched by the sweep of Frank's headlights
across the yard, as we drop Walt,
a dozen beers and yelps, passed out,
face down in the snarled fronds.
Even in the dark there's more of you
than us, and I know the hard frost

will never stop your frantic stems,
my mother's spade, the thick
grapple-hooks of your roots.
What the fuck am I doing?—waiting
for the kitchen light to die,
standing, half-drunk, half-kid,
in a kingdom of pachysandra.

Stray Dogs, Foaming

The poor man has misplaced the silk
    fingers his father wove. Dry rot
splits the joist and shingles crack.
    The sick woman has drunk a river.
Still, fires in her body popple and jet.
    Not all are guilty, but all
are responsible, Dostoevski said.
    Our clocks keep their jobs, and we walk
with efficient prophets. Come autumn
    the hemlock will take the laurel.
What to do with old Styrofoam,
    the cowbird stealing the finch's nest.
When the battered kid blows his flute,
    only stray dogs hear the sound.
They rush through dark streets,
    mouths foaming. The air has always
been scratched, the water swollen.
    And as much as we'd like to believe
otherwise, we aren't the first to wake
    with wounds we thought sleep would salve.

Vasectomy

for Adam Smith

No one's notified the workers
special dividends have been issued,
the factory sold. Frames
are still being welded, transmissions
bolted to engines, acetylene torches lit
gold like the light from miners' helmets
on groaning timber. Coal
is still chiseled and dust
spun into lungs. No one's posted signs:
Road Out. Bridge Out. Danger Ahead.
Fingers black with dye, young girls
disappear in looms. Women
boil metal, pour it steaming into molds.
Day fused to night, millions of laborers,
backs crooked and hands cracked,
manufacture bottles, canisters and cogs,
replicating product
that will never reach foreign markets.
Soldiers turn semis back at the border.
Executives charter planes,
shift funds into Swiss accounts.
How long before word of this
hits the factories, the mines, the wicked
textile mills? What good, what possible good,
is supply without demand?

On Being Kicked Out of the Harold Washington Library Center for Napping on the Floor

Above me no seraphim or nymphs,
but crew-cut men, walkie-talkies, crisp
uniforms, the tallest saying
Sir, you'll have to leave.
This room with its mahogany clock,
azure lights, dozens of new chairs
set in perfect lines, the grain
smooth as vowels. Hunched
over tables a few students
scribble notes, others thumb pages
and everywhere the smell
of fresh wax. Down four flights
we march, one in front and one
behind, past portraits of dour
Chicago fathers, frescoes splashed
with lilies and nudes, past
magazines, blunt newspapers,
the willowy librarian
hovering pictures above children, banished
from this province of books,
dear James I too
have wasted my life.

Each Saturday After

double knots below the shins,
cement floors and rubber mats,
they clop on the ice—hard nail of water
buffed to a perfect gloss.
Teachers, mechanics, waitresses,
accountants and C-trick workers,
orbiting like planets around the rink's
red circles. Near the boards
the young couple catch each other,
push off again. Little boys
with wooden sticks and helmets
hear a whistle. They whisk over the ice,
stop and shred it on the next blast.
A bearded man, gloves in his pockets,
glides. Purple socks and bow
looks down for assurance.
Her older sisters race, loop
by the tall, turtleneck parents
holding the hands of their kid
who chops, skitters and is yanked
first north and then south.
By the orange pylons two girls,
legs wide as wickets, skate backwards,
while a man traces figure-eights,
knees bent, arms stretched.
Around and around they go.
Parkas and sharp blades,
laughing, talking, yelling to someone
in the bleachers where I sit, no doubt
where you've sat, to watch them
cross-step and lean through an edge,
chasing after who they've been

if not what they might be
in this place that they trust
will get them back to where they are.

The Other Body

Slick-wet from the bath
our infant lies on the carpet
kicking bubbles of sun.
Pine boughs bob in sudden wind.
Down the street a girl opens
her journal, her father
wrenches the oil pan's bolt.

Leaf. Salt shaker. Nail.
Each fragment known to itself
despite our assumptions.
Yellow Jackets stun the air.
Mud shifts and the furnace
thumps. We blink,
suffer for cohesion,

crouching by the tracks
deer leave on the hill.
How evasive the other body,
how much work.
Place a foot to test the quickening
water. Here is a small boat
with oars of different size.

The End Won't Be So Bad

The Man with a New Toothbrush

has moves unfamiliar to anyone else,
stiff bristles and the savvy
to negotiate bicuspids, the slick
chasms between molars. His partnership
with fluoride more spontaneous
collaboration than long-term contract,

as he cuts loose from floss, his gums'
incessant appeals. There's no reason
to squeeze paste from the bottom.
Why, even the mirror is superfluous,
each sweep, bringing him closer
to his original jaw, is a gesture
against Novocain, silver instruments

wrapped in a towel. He knows tartar
is only self-aggrandized plaque,
that for too long we've been terrified
of canines, their midnight transformations. . . .
The man with a new toothbrush
sits down for a little snack, masticates

glucose and starch, a thousand preservatives,
and sated, slowly napkins his lips, burps
and pulls a winter coat
around his body, his body
of pure enamel and bone, steps
through the revolving door into a squall,
a whiteout, smiling.

The Woman with a Full Tank

of super unleaded cares little
for maps, the odometer, all those
whatchamacallits diminished in a rearview
glance, is rarely assuaged by billboards,
the light flashing red or the lane

that appears when traveling
sharp hills, so many rural miles
of static and country singers
mourning the finale of girlfriends, trucks,
their mommas and their dogs.

High test octane and black
nail polish. She'd rather think
about distance and speed, how the clutch
catapults toward fifth, how pervasive
the smell of fresh tar in June

when it's easy to push the engine
through curves, past a jumble
of road signs she's apt to ignore
though there've been passive moments
in history, a few. Let someone else

collect the scattered pieces
of rubber from commercial rigs, worry
about gunk on the sparks,
rest rooms, whitetail, Kuwait.
It's just a Dodge and a woman

without a plot, no associates
and plenty of fuel, *sustenance*
in the fourth Webster's definition,
her favorite, and so cruises
all night over asphalt, macadam

and never stops out of hunger
or some nostalgia for where she was.
Two fingers on the wheel. A foot
on the dash. Even the wind
can't predict her next move.

White Birds

The iron has done all it could.
His dress shirts hang in the closet.
They are white birds and the branches
of poplars stripped of leaves.
And still they are shirts.
Collars, buttons and cuffs
filed along with the jackets.
This one is a speech he wrote
for shareholders in Florida. This
a multimedia show: slides and film,
three-by-five flash cards
for the chairman of the board.
He doesn't know I've come to look;
to touch the tin discs
of cordovan and black;
to open, then close the wooden box
that is home to the cloths
heavy with years of polish.
The silver rack on the door
holds belts and fat ties
he hasn't worn since Nixon.
He's put shoe trees in his wingtips,
laid them side by side. Small coffins.
Tomorrow, my father will wake
at the first crease of light.
He will shower and towel,
hitch, fasten and straighten,
check each pleat, each button,
bend and tie the shoes
that will tap the slick,
buffed floors, as he walks

toward executive suites,
briefcase in hand,
to prove the labor of his hours.

In the Interest of Possibility

a young engineer receives a wooden crate marked: *unusual cargo handle with care.*

    At the eastern slope of a garden
    snow falls where a cherry tree has perished.

He asked for a slice of the West, and his mother-in-law delivered.

    Against the dead bark the old samurai
    sits and knows his life has filled enough days.

With this tumbleweed, he'll have something, come summer,
to roll across the yard.

    Running in the garden, children stop and snap
    their fingers, but the old man doesn't blink.

One more thing with shit stuck to it is his wife's reply.

    Quickly, the dagger sends the samurai's ghost
    into the tree.

Two hours after making love, they dig at the frozen ground,
drop manure in a cart.

    Each year people travel hundreds of miles
    to stand in thick sweeps of snow while
    the cherry blossoms open.

What could be better, he says, than a beer, a lawn chair,
and a good tumbleweed.

Huddled, they watch and dream of crushed
fruit, breast milk.

She reminds him that amaranths scratch, and this weed
in the hands of their kids will be trouble.

It is the 16th of January.

It is the 19th of March.

A pink star flares
at the eastern slope of a garden.

The Rottweilers sniff, squat.

As This Is Our Century

the spruce have a pact with rain
they trust won't be broken.
When the bruised potato asks
for a different costume, the butter
offers its gold dress. In school
we learn how a single agent
determines a response, how the wires
hung above roads translate power
even when we can't pay our bills,
all of us trapped in aluminum
foil, some tonic recommended
by specialists and the notion
of emeralds without dragons.
Yet, every so often we hear
about the woman who climbs
into her instrument and discovers
a forgotten tone, and this helps
us remember that charity
is the quotient of compassion
divided by perspective, ours
or anyone else who calls
on the last of their strength
to expel what arrives as boredom,
indifference, razing this derelict
house for a rumor of the place
where each thing has two handles, one
by which it may be held
and the other by which it cannot.

Swimmers

We are swimming. In rivers, oceans, lakes,
from the shore to the island, from the dock
to the raft, by the quay where the ships
bring their haul. We are swimming
like dolphins, puppies, the salmon
we once were, up streams and down
brooks, in the neighbor's above-ground pool,
whipkicking and fluttering, taking
quick bites of air while the thunder
closes and cranes dredge the channel.
We are swimming through the kettle's blue eye,
the bayou's green reeds, donning trunks and caps,
nylon racing suits, our buttocks pumping
like the pistons in outboards, the engines
in barges heavy with their cities of trash.
We are swimming, blowing jets of water clear
as champagne, paddling beneath the lifeguard's
silver glasses, splashing *Marco Polo, Jacques Cousteau*,
treading under waterfalls, in bays and ponds,
goosebumps and our lips rainbowed
like the oil staining feathers and rocks,
the thick nets of kelp, the water cold
from the mountain, hot from the spring,
plankton and PCB, our nipples fat as starfish.
We are swimming in Olympic pools,
gullies and swamps, yelping in old creeks
reconfigured by bulldozers,
side-stroking and back-floating,
our fingers wrinkled, our skin wrapped
in white grease. We are swimming
without webs, gills, pectoral fins
as the sewers run and the culverts spit,
butterfly and frogkick, the preservers tight

around our necks, knowing
that one ounce in one lung,
knowing buoys sink, breakwalls give.
We are swimming, in rivers and in oceans,
the good neighbor's above-ground pool,
though the chlorine stings, the salt cakes,
the lifeguard shouts: All right. Everybody
out of the water!

Going on the Belief Walleyes Eat Late

we fish at dusk. No strikes.
Just the occasional bass
thwapping the roof of the water,
making us wish our boat
were anywhere but here.
Which is the umbrella bed—
fat sandbar of stalk weeds, shells,
tangled hooks and lures,
the snouts of old centerboards.

We've nailed some giants off this bed.
Speckled green, dorsal fins bristled,
they died in the snarl of our net.
The thought of those fish
can tease a mile of line from a reel.
So we let out a little more
as the lake goes black and the loon
cries to its mate. The locals say
when you can't see the end of your pole
the day is done.

Tacit

The ice and the scotch, the fable
and the farce, three diamonds,
two no trump, Moe's fingers
and Curly's sockets,
what the judge expects, the plaintiff
seeks, remora and shark,
noose and neck, Rubens' brush
and the frost on the polders,
their tabby and the couch,
our poodle and his balls,
this knife, that piece
of muffin wedged
between the coils, a neighbor's
lamppost, a boy's slingshot,
how the tux stratifies, the bra
enhances, album, cassette, compact
disc, the mold and the grout,
the march and the Mace,
his bonds, her stocks,
my last legitimate
maneuver, my next
felonious thought.

God's Enigmatic Silence

puzzles no more than the pavement
that runs out of itself
at the end of our village, the flies
who walk about the ceiling

in redundant circles without
cell phones or Birkenstocks.
The instructions warn against sleeping
near the microwave, except

in October when so many trees
are asked to make ambiguous
decisions. Think of what we might
accomplish with the vim

of a Bach thirty-second note.
It's difficult to finish these
blue book tests where
you don't have the option

to stutter, to check the column
all of the above. Tell me, if you will,
about the monks at matins
during the tremors crushed

by blocks of plaster
upon which were painted
priceless renaissance frescoes,
how life is fleeting, art elegiac, or

is it, perchance, the other way around?

The Revisionist at Work

From the sill he lifts the clay pots
of begonias, the sugar bowl, the spoon,
takes a cloth and wipes the dust
off the wood that no longer

reconciles the paint, the paint
peeled and cracked, bubbled
at the corners of mullions,
and folding a piece of extra

fine paper, the force of his index
and thumb on its edge, sands
and sands and sands, a vigorous
motion over the uneven surfaces

which frame each cube of glass,
white flecks on his nails, white
motes in the air, sands
until the paper is exhausted,

the task unfinished, requiring
more sheets and so descends
the steps to the cellar
with its mildew and webs,

puddles on the floor, cold
cement, that place where he fetches
the slab of veal, the mousetraps,
caulk for the tile, poison

for the weeds, trying to convince
himself that he won't return
even as he knows
there's little doubt that he will.

Faster

And he whom you cannot teach to fly,
teach to fall faster.

—Friedrich Nietzsche

Seventy in the left lane, four miles
to O'Hare we pass a blue
shuttle bus, its exigent
hazards, one tire deflated,
precarious as guilt. From a window
a woman makes frantic gestures. . . .

Billboards and lacerated brick
apartments, hawkweeds brush
the shins of speed limit signs.
On a bridge someone has painted
Read Swedenborg   And You Shall Know
Last night hundreds of people

camped in the park, watched
workers hammer scaffolds, test mikes
for today's championship
rally. The body asks the soul
but the soul has gone out
in search of a rumor of itself.

At the airport a white button sends
plastic around the toilet seat,
protecting us from others.
Why so ravenous to praise
a few men who toss
a ball through a net?

Attendants slam carryon bins, check
belts. We wait our turn. Bloodshot,
her eyes were more salmon
than carp. From suspended televisions
Republicans blast the President—
obstruction of justice—

promise new investigations, the wind
off the lake committed
to raking clouds. Can eighteen million
over three years pull
a camel through a needle?
I did not urge the cabby to stop.

Only the Traveler Can Change the Journey

is how we convince ourselves
these days though sometimes
we look elsewhere, think
to reassemble you, fog-
thrumming man fast to shift
through four A.M. piles of poems,
all sky and juniper, the trout
quicksilvering the brook.
And the question of solitude
has always been answered
by one pine needle
refusing to fall. What remains:
hard as redwood, the deep bite
of axe. Ferns where your feet
moved slow and far from people.
In August the light
lies down like an elk
for the river, the hills, this
earth that we touch,
old friend, it lies down.

(in memory of William Stafford)

The End Won't Be So Bad

the dead get away with most anything.
They leave the knife in the mustard,
the lamps burning hot,
garage doors open for the flies, as the dead
have no allegiance to food or light,
and certainly not to garbage nor the graves
where we bring our scarlet roses
never suspecting that the dead
have gone down the street
to shoot tequila at McDermott's,
chalk cues with lonely husbands
sealed in the plum-colored smoke.
Bar maids bring pretzels, the next round
of bourbon. The musk of old beers, oak tabletops.
The dead feed quarters to the blushing juke,
push shot glasses like shuffleboard disks.
This is how they love to be,
among the tittle-tattle and bravado,
laying wagers on which cardigan
will draw sparks from the nearest skirt,
that spontaneous combustion of fabric
in a bar or in the wash. The dead believe
there's no point in separating
the colors from the whites, in flossing
every molar, balancing checks.
They prefer to run their fingers
over the cat's sleek coat or flick
the butterflies above the crib,
that strange flutter which makes us stop,
whisper a little lie about the dead,
how they move through our bodies
like sleigh-runners through snow,

how they sneak downstairs
to eat the last chocolate torte,
dead set, just like us,
on getting away with most anything.

Spin Cycle

Black Forests

You've come down the stairs this snow-whipped
dawn, your robe unhitched, hair matted
and slippers flopping, to the living room, still cold,
and the couch, a mess of papers, pencils and me,
to ask, in a small voice, if I'll stop and help.
I will. For I believe in goblins, those wild
black forests as much as your
dead grandmother, she of runes and charms,
a wool kerchief wrapped around
one-hundred-six Ukrainian years,
who showed you, without a whisper of English,
what you've showed me, that I do,
now: pushing back your stray curls;
cradling your neck; lowering my head;
pursing both lips against the swale
of your ear, as I close my eyes
and fill my lungs, completely,
pause, and then, blow once without force,
but sure enough so that
this scoop of air clatters among
the hammer and stirrup, swoops
through the dark tunnel, the spiraling nautilus.
One breath to chase away
what was up all night walking in your head.
Sweetheart, when this little wind
snares your daemon you'll go back to sleep,
as your Baba said, as you did
those first winter mornings while the ice
trapped the house, and you dozed
on her lap, a drop
of her woodsmoke breath in your ear.

Water Baby

Tie-dye bandana. Jeff Airplane June.
The girl hip deep in the fountain,
in the photo, in the middle
of the park, is my wife. Only

she doesn't know it,
yet. But she does know
how to sport cutoffs
for the camera, how to enjoy
violating city code number

nine   seven   four
not to be confused with
nineteen   seven   one
printed on Kodachrome,
the silver emulsion gone egg-creme

from the heat. No doubt
George Eastman would shoot
the last black rhino
if it meant he could move
the lens of his fingers

over her cocoa-melt skin.
But that's an exposure
no one can develop,
as George has checked in
to the big dark room.

And she's here, the sun
outside the frame relentless,
the whirlpools nuzzling up
to her thighs—this girl
paddling the bubbles as if

she might linger forever.
Who could blame her?
Who wouldn't dawdle?—
allow the water to turn
nipples into pennies,

like the thousand copper flashes
she sees but cannot hear,
wishes long since tossed and waiting
for answers, for the chance to love
any crazy-wave, fountain-froth girl.

Regarding Shoulders

You can begin anywhere—
a scarf, knapsack, the sergeant's
black chevrons, feathers spread
from neck to arm is a peacock
your drunk brother let
his buddy tattoo one night,
the bull in Les Jemison's field
grazing timothy, his shoulders
two small trucks, pads
for the linebacker, a red dress
rivering across the bar, each strap
little more than a trickle of lipstick,
your Swedish aunt in the pantry
leveling dough, all of her brawn
frontloaded. It's possible
that beneath our flesh, our
spindled muscle, one blade's
a granite block from New Hampshire,
the other some easy green, languid
as Vermont. However shoulders move
it's not far from comb or brush,
those glistening webs of hair
left on the pillow at dawn,
so we might ask—
*can I cry on your? has she turned
a cold?* giving what we have
straight from, putting it,
like they say, to the wheel
of the Plymouth, driving
to a funeral or reunion
through sleet, spattering rain,
low on gas and in a town
we've never seen before, from nowhere

struck by a rogue necessity
to search the cramped, dilapidated
neighborhoods for the blistered house
we left years back in another town,
rope swing and dandelions, the road's
gold hyphen dragging us on—
go, go, go, wipers slushing, the van
in the mirror blasting its horn
is enough to make us forget
to begin any place,
a scarf or knapsack, a strip
of wet tarmac where
we could pull over, cut the ignition,
unhitch our belt, turn
to the woman or man
sleeping next to us, and lightly,
ever so lightly, feather our lips
over cheek, neck, blunted wing.

Spin Cycle

When the dial reaches lock and spin, the machine
shakes like a drunken angel,
joggles its plastic cylinders, aluminum walls,
the hidden rivers of electricity.
That and the effort carried out
by the neighboring dryer, generate tremors
as I hoist you to the white metal,
raise your favorite skirt
in the not-quite-dark, ease you
against the slope of the panel
where we choose how much and how warm.
Scattered pennies on the rug, high boots
over my shoulders, most of you
pushing against me, the rumble of sweaters,
flannels, tie-dye T-shirts, froth
and pockets of trapped air in the chasm
below. It's as near to the naked
truth as we'll get, that
there's no escaping the world's
little tempests, no place on the map
for The Red Cross to respond,
though I hope with enough moxie and all
that's possible with finesse
we'll accomplish some measure
of ourselves even as we risk what
might conceivably shrink,
might fade. Your smile has curled
into a thread, the scarlet tip
of a fingernail. This machine
knows our rhythm.
I'm holding on to your heels.

Sandy Lake, Late August

The weather is what the wind is.
And today the wind shifts faster
than the mottled gulls snatching minnows
she tears from her hook and tosses

to the green water. How quickly
those limp bodies go. Without a ripple.
The birds know we're good for more,
silver bucket slapping

against the hip of the boat.
I reach in, curl my fingers.
The minnows are cool, moist, elastic.
They twist and avoid my grasp. . . .

It would be nothing to sink
this pail, watch the water race,
the backwash sweep them out
like a cloud of opals.

The Fax

is the vagabond in a black coat
with a secret. Touch a button and wait.
Try not to confuse it
for something else, although

like sex, the body politic, we drop
a fax on someone as we would
our tongue or a bomb. Dynamics shift
and influence expectations. Once

we've faxed another it's difficult
to return to phone. India and Pakistan.
We test who's beyond our vision
while the paper negotiates the slot.

What's the likelihood of faxus interruptus?
What words will excite the Palestinians
and not upset the Jews? All of us
moving from lover to lover, from fax

to nuke, determined to get there first.
Because it's possible that history
is only the perpetual relay
of invention, Eros and power,

and our task is to wait on the street
for the vagabond to hand us
the glossy page, that message we sent
to warn ourselves of what we might become.

Barbara

This morning there's no grass
by the white river of bed between us.
But since I am a water snake,
I slither, roll on my side and pull
the warm of you to the cold of me.
Now, your spine is sheathed in my chest,
your nape moist against my face, your legs
clamping my knees, this figure we make
of silence and balance. I flash
my tongue along your shoulder,
brush my fingers over your hip, slopes
that keep shifting. Your thighs and breasts
could be drumlins, kames,
your nipples the smooth stones
I find along the path, your hair so thick
scouts with compasses would vanish.
Forgive me, it's selfish to act like this
when you're exhausted, to stroke your skin,
clasp the pouch where our third,
in his cumulus bubble, sleeps,
as you are trying to sleep, now
that your legs have begun to ache,
your pelvic bones separating,
two wings loosening for the passage
of this child, who is river and cloud,
snake and bird, yet mostly, you, a woman
numinous as the water
in each cloud, each river,
abiding all that comes to you,
even thoughtlessness borne from love,
a man's gaze, a man's touch, *this*.

Honeysuckle Bower

If I die here on my back
looking up at the vines
everything will remain
as it is: fat leaves, lobed flowers,
bees stitching the heat, plump
as the penises of two-year-olds.

I wouldn't dare
put one in my mouth.
And yet to be stung—
to feel the black dart
work deep, draw blood.

If I go like nectar
from honeysuckle,
drop by drop, I will dream
of my wife at my nipple,
little blimps, wafer wings, sweet
bloated vowels.

Anaphoric

to my wife on our tenth

Because it is easy to lie,
    to say we write
from pleasure and not fear
    of the indeterminate.
Because the wheat that's withstood
    so much wind
cares little for the blade.
    Because the mantis
cloaks, the heron strikes,
    the key
shares its secret with the knob.
    All truths
wait in all things, Whitman said.
    They neither hasten
their own delivery nor resist it.
    Who wouldn't
want to believe that, and who
    wouldn't challenge
such reckless assertion. Clearly,
    we cannot stop
the lights on automatic timers,
    the rain that fails
to slow the heat, extinguish
    our humid
inclinations, each strength
    a weakness,
hour into hour into ana-
    phoric hour.
Because how often we forget
    that art is only
a portal to love, that the waiting

is work, that one
strident move will deliver us
        from sweetheart
to son-of-a-bitch.

Walking Down This Mountain

I'm coming home
a little crazier than the maples,
those maidens by the house gathering
their butterscotch skirts,
their arms generous
with the first October frost.
I'm dizzy as those trees
that dip and spin
in the light off the porch,
like the girl
just back from the grange,
who danced, drank
the thick sugary punch
that made her tongue a red leaf,
made it glow in his mouth—
the boy down the street, pulsing
with more fire than he began.

The Bar Beyond the World

is where you wait, drink while Simon Peter
    and his seraphim
review your papers. Hard to believe

you'd have it so good, that limbo would include
    a vinyl stool,
cold drafts in tall glasses, the beer

slipping through this image of your body
    with the speed
of fresh gossip, no breathalyzers, hangovers.

Why waffle on whether to stop or swig
    one more, now that time
and alcohol have no influence, as you sit

between the salesman you turned away
    in eighty-nine, the woman
who called looking for the Humane Society

and pissed at your boss you barked
    twice, hung up. Her
daughter, so courteous checking your tickets

in Rome, who never touched a drop
    yet failed to steer
her coupe away from the truck, four whiskey-

thick boys, is here doing shots, singing
    ballads with Jack
Reynolds, otherwise known as Inspector 513

who spent his days making sure the cotton
    Jockeys you adored
held their shape, never ripped; beyond

them Absolut and Clarence, years mopping
    floors at your church,
in charge of liquid soap, toilet paper;

while Gladys Baron, the albino teller
    you always stared at,
shares a bottle of Chablis with Linda Choe

who delivered bills, fat letters to your door
    each noon. And isn't
that the lawyer quick to relinquish

his aisle seat to your wife, the clerk
    who let you purchase
the clothes washer on bad credit,

laughing over daiquiris, greasy baskets
    of fries on this sweep
of mahogany where you share old

bourbon, a few spicy jokes with people
    who were small
felicities, chance encounters, easy targets

for the poison darts of your indifference,
    the anger that was
a portion of the life you were compelled

to live, the life assessed by those
    who hold dominion,
as this guy in a Texaco cap

who long ago on Buckhorn Lake divulged
    the spot where the muskies
hit, hands you a bowl of cashews,

macadamia nuts, and suddenly all you desire
    is that Peter, his
righteous associates, scrupulously weighing

everything you achieved against what you lost,
    that they, despite their ethereal
wisdom, find it impossible to reach a verdict.

Thanks to Bill Heyen, for listening and believing, to Bill Tremblay, Tony Piccione, Stan Rubin, "Freddy" Poulin, Judith Kitchen, Stephen Dunn, DeLoss McGraw and Richard Foerster, to The Take No Prisoners Poetry Gang: Mary Jo Iuppa, Susan Holahan, Jim Hancock and Jane Schuster who bloodied their hands with some of these poems, and to Jerry Costanzo and the staff at Carnegie Mellon University Press.

* * *

"Shopping with Henry David Thoreau" is for Greg Gale & Michael Lasser. "Going on the Belief Walleyes Eat Late" is for Barton Sutter. "In the Interest of Possibility" is for Shelley & Larry Davis. "The Revisionist at Work" is for Steve Huff. "God's Enigmatic Silence" is for Laure-Anne Bosselaar. "Everywhere, Pachysandra" is for Jim Erwin & Rob Terhune. "Dark Underfoot" is for our kids.